Merseyside in Monochrome

Priestley and Sons, Merseyside Photographers

The story of a Victorian and Edwardian family business

by

Mike Priestley

First Published 2010 by Countyvise Limited,
14 Appin Road, Birkenhead, Wirral CH41 9HH

Copyright © 2010 Mike Priestley

The right of Mike Priestley to be identified as the editor of this work has been asserted by him in accordance with the Copyright, Design and Patents Act 1988.

The rights of the individual authors to be identified as the author of their work has been asserted by them in accordance with the Copyright, Design and Patents Act 1988.

British Library Cataloguing in Publication Data.
A catalogue record for this book is available from the British Library.

ISBN 978 1 906823 35 1

Foreword

This book is dedicated to my father.

Gordon Priestley [1908-1996] was the only son of Arthur Priestley and grandson of Samuel Stansfield Priestley. As a young man he occasionally worked as an assistant to his father, carrying heavy photographic equipment to various assignments in Wallasey, but he was never tempted to be further involved in the company's activities.

The bulk of this collection of photos and the other documents referred to, survived in his safe keeping for over half a century.

Mike Priestley   18/10/2008

Contents

Introduction

In Huddersfield

The Priestleys were a Yorkshire family. Samuel Stansfield Priestley was born in Bradford in 1826, the son of William Lee Priestley [1803-1876] and Hannah Mary Priestley, formerly Knott, [1806-1888]. Sam married Sarah Ann Maud [1830-1874] and together they had 8 children, 4 boys and 4 girls, one of whom, Ada, died in infancy. The family lived at 30, Manchester Road, Huddersfield, which still stands, where Sam worked as a tailor. In 1856 Sam started a photography business, which went on to occupy a number of different premises in the town over the next 28 years. There is evidence for the existence of the following studios during that time:

St Peter's Street	1861-4
Back John William Street/Church Street	1866-70
Swan Yard, Kirkgate	1867-71
Wood Street	1870-1
58, New Street	1872-5
56, New Street	1875-6
28, Ramsden Street	1876-81

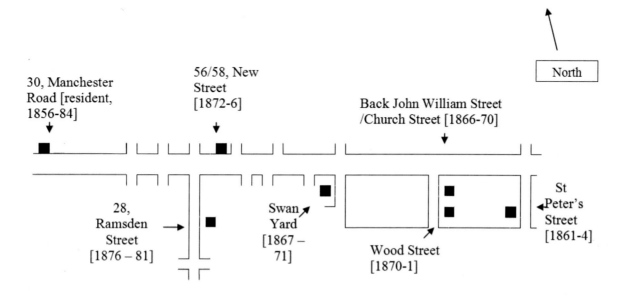

Map to show the approximate locations of the Huddersfield studios of Samuel Stansfield Priestley [not to scale]

Advertisements in the Huddersfield Directory in 1873 and 1876 promoted the business, with Sam emphasizing his ability to enlarge small photographs to lifesize, finishing them in oil or water colour and presenting them on canvas. They were known as oleographs. He also advertised the sale of picture frames, albums, scrap books, screen pictures and highly finished miniatures on ivory, paper or porcelain. Reductions were on offer for "quantities of Cartes or Cabinet Pictures".

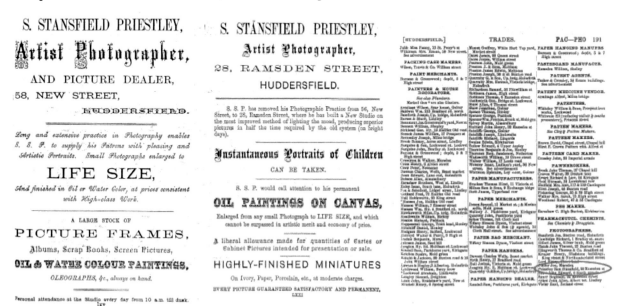

Advertisements in the Huddersfield Directory [1-1873, 2-1876, 3-1881]. By 1881 Samuel had competition from Reginald Spurr close by in Ramsden Street. Perhaps this was another factor encouraging him to make the move to Merseyside just 3 years later.

In 1871 the family comprised:

Samuel Priestley, Head of household, aged 44, born Bradford
Sarah Ann Priestley, wife, aged 40, born Stanningley
Hannah Mary Priestley, daughter, unmarried, aged 18, born Bradford
Alice Maud Mary Priestley, daughter, aged 16, born Huddersfield
James Priestley, son, aged 14, scholar, born Huddersfield
William Priestley, son, aged 11, scholar, born Huddersfield
Joseph Priestley, son, aged 9, scholar, born Huddersfield
Arthur Priestley, son, aged 7, scholar, born Huddersfield
Elizabeth Priestley, daughter, aged 4, born Huddersfield

By the time of the 1881 census Sam was working in Ramsden Street as a photographer, with Hannah as his assistant. Joseph and Arthur were employed as woollen warehousemen and James was at the Post Office. Also in the household at Manchester Road were:

Anne Marie Bentley, aged 73, dressmaker, born Kirkstall
Emma Dutton, aged 50, servant, born Kirkstall
Rebecca Jeffrey, aged 40, sister-in law, born Stanningley

Rebecca was the sister of Sam's wife, Sarah, who had died in 1874, at the age of 44.

The Priestley connection with Huddersfield ended in 1884 so it is perhaps no surprise that there is little to record about the business and its fortunes before then. Sam's name is mentioned in a list of Victorian photographers who produced cartes de visite and as such is represented in the archives of The National Portrait Gallery, which possesses an image of the Reverend Josiah Bateman. The Reverend Bateman was vicar at St Peter's Parish Church in Huddersfield, a short walk from Sam's studio in the centre of the town.

Very few pictures are known to have survived from this era. The oldest item in the collection is a daguerreotype [or one of the similar glass positive images developed around the same time]. It is mounted in a glazed and ornately carved wooden frame. On the rear is the inscription:

"GREAT GREAT Grandmother DINAH. [LEE .] Wife of Jonathan Priestley. Mother of William Lee Priestley, Grandmother of Sam Stansfield Priestley, Great grandmother of William Priestley". Dinah died in 1858 so the picture is at least 150 years old.

Other remaining pictures from the period are :

- A cartes de visite sized positive image on glass of an unnamed girl [possibly an ambrotype or a result of the application of the collodian process].
- "William Priestley [Father of S.S.P.] Died 19.1.1876 Aged 73 years. Buried in Huddersfield Cemetery".
- 2 of "Mrs William Priestley [nee Knott] Mother of S.S.P. Born 7.6.1806 Died 22.12.1888. Buried in Huddersfield Cemetery".
- A miniature of "Mrs John Collier [Grandmother of Mrs A. Priestley"].
- An unmarked print of William Priestley.
- One named photograph of Samuel Priestley.
- One of " Mrs S.S. Priestley [nee Maud] B 31.5.1830 D 9.3.74 Buried in Huddersfield Cemetery".
- 4 miniatures of Arthur Priestley as a young man.

- 1 miniature of young Jimmie Priestley.
- A view of the Swan Yard studio with "Priestley's Photographic Studio", barely legible above the door.

The only known photograph of Samuel's business premises in Swan Yard, off Kirkgate, in the centre of the town.

William Priestley, 1803-1876, father of Samuel Stansfield Priestley.

An early print taken from the only surviving daguerreotype image in the Priestley collection. It shows Dinah Lee, 1782-1858, who was reputed to be of gypsy stock. Dinah was married to Jonathan Priestley, 1778-1850, who was the grandfather of Samuel Stansfield Priestley.

Samuel Stansfield Priestley, founder of the photographic business of Priestley and Sons in Huddersfield in 1856.

A collection of cartes de visite of members of the family from the Huddersfield era showing:-

Mrs John Collier, Grandmother of Mrs A. Priestley. [Sarah Ann Maud, 1830-1874, was Samuel's wife]

Jimmie Priestley, 1856-1926

Arthur Priestley, 1863-1940, as a child

Three of Arthur Priestley as a young man. Arthur went on to run the business on Merseyside after his father's death.

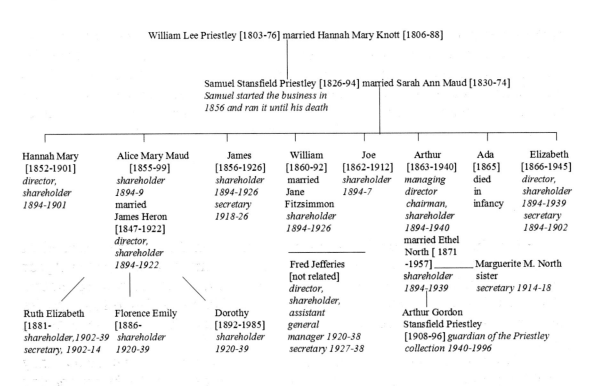

William Lee Priestley [1803-76] married Hannah Mary Knott [1806-88]

Samuel Stansfield Priestley [1826-94] married Sarah Ann Maud [1830-74]
*Samuel started the business in
1856 and ran it until his death*

Hannah Mary
[1852-1901]
*director,
shareholder
1894-1901*

Alice Mary Maud
[1855-99]
*shareholder
1894-9
married
James Heron
[1847-1922]
director,
shareholder
1894-1922*

James
[1856-1926]
*shareholder
1894-1926
secretary
1918-26*

William
[1860-92]
*married
Jane
Fitzsimmon
shareholder
1894-1926*

Joe
[1862-1912]
*shareholder
1894-7*

Arthur
[1863-1940]
*managing
director
chairman,
shareholder
1894-1940
married Ethel
North [1871
-1957]
shareholder
1894-1939*

Ada
[1865]
*died
in
infancy*

Elizabeth
[1866-1945]
*director,
shareholder
1894-1939
secretary
1894-1902*

Marguerite M. North
sister
secretary 1914-18

Fred Jefferies
[not related]
*director,
shareholder,
assistant
general
manager 1920-38
secretary 1927-38*

Ruth Elizabeth
[1881-
*shareholder,1902-39
secretary, 1902-14*

Florence Emily
[1886-
*shareholder
1920-39*

Dorothy
[1892-1985]
*shareholder
1920-39*

Arthur Gordon
Stansfield Priestley
[1908-96] *guardian of the Priestley
collection 1940-1996*

Part of the Priestley family tree to show positions in the company.

Page one of a notebook recording, alphabetically, photographs taken by the company. It gives print sizes and the picture catalogue numbers, which are often visible along the bottom of the photographs.

Page one of a notebook recording photographs taken by the company, in a numbered sequence. It indicates print size and contains occasional, apposite remarks. The list is not, however, directly related to chronological ordering and some additional information has clearly been added at later dates than the original entries.

In 1884 the family left Huddersfield and moved to Merseyside. They hoped to take advantage of the expansion of the port and city of Liverpool and the opportunities that a rapidly growing population might provide for them. The original business in Huddersfield remains a bit of a mystery. Appeals through the local press there have come up with little that is new. Research has confirmed and clarified, without uncovering any treasure trove of forgotten pictures.

In Wallasey

On their arrival on Merseyside Samuel's son Arthur was installed at Medrington's Photographers, of 29a, Bold Street, Liverpool, to complete a 2 year apprenticeship. The first studio in Wallasey was at 17, Falkland Road, Egremont, which was also home to many of the family. Samuel Priestley died in 1894 and the transfer of the firm's headquarters to 1, Falkland Road took place in the following year.

At this time it was decided by Arthur and the rest of the family that they should set up a limited company. Arthur Priestley became the first managing director. Miss Hannah Mary Priestley and Miss Elizabeth Priestley were directors and shareholders. Elizabeth was also appointed secretary. The other original members included James Heron [1847-1922], an architect, who was Sam's son in law, married to Alice Mary Maud Priestley. James Priestley was chairman. Joseph Priestley, who had emigrated to Australia, was a shareholder, as were Jane Fitzsimmon Priestley, [the widow of William Priestley, who had died in 1892] and Arthur's wife, Ethel North Priestley.

The affairs of the limited company throughout the period are recorded in a book containing the hand written minutes of the annual general and shareholders' meetings. Also included are the typed balance sheets for each financial year, provided by the auditors Simon, Jude and West, who were employed throughout the company's existence. These documents give a clear indication of the fluctuating fortunes of the company.

Most of the reports are fairly brief affairs. They contain conventional balance sheets, which record working profits and losses on an annual basis. These show, for example, that in 1897 dividends

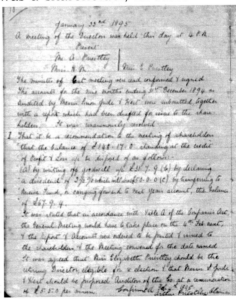

The hand written minutes of the first annual general meeting of the limited company, on 4th February 1895.

The company's final annual report was prepared for the last A.G.M. held on 31st March 1938. The complete and meticulous account of the company's affairs ends abruptly here. It was followed a year later by a Balance Sheet and Trading and Profit and Loss Account, which effectively wound up the business.

paid to shareholders had doubled to 10% and that they increased again the next year to 15%. In the same year the company bought the photographic business of W. Clement Davis, of 32, Balls Road, Claughton for £400. This became known as the Claughton branch in company documents thereafter.

The Report of Directors, dated 21st January 1900, showed a "profit on the year's working [for 1899] of £234 14s. 5d." The company entered the twentieth century with apparently sound finances and justifiable optimism. Samuel Priestley had successfully transferred his photographic business from Huddersfield to Wallasey and his son, Arthur, had become well established in the area at the head of the limited company which was working out of 2 studios. Sam's eldest son James [1856-1926] and his youngest daughter Elizabeth [1866-1945] also worked in the family firm and they lived in a first floor flat above the main studio at 1, Falkland Road.

The surviving comprehensive documentation of the company, in the handwriting of successive secretaries, plots the fluctuations in fortunes, which turned into a battle for survival as the decades passed. The 1900 report was favourable, "especially considering that most photographic businesses have suffered considerably during the year, owing to the continuance of the war in South Africa". The 1901 report records the death and the loss to the company of Miss Hannah Mary Priestley, during the preceding year. The next year Ruth Heron took over as secretary from Elizabeth Priestley.

The report for 1903 recorded the first loss in the company's history and mentioned the transfer of the Claughton branch from Balls Road to a studio at Columbia House, 13, Shrewsbury Road, Oxton, which also became the family home for a short time. Within a year, an operating profit had reduced the debit but had not wiped it out and

Arthur Priestley and his wife, formerly Ethel North, with their dog, Metz, in their garden at 13, Shrewsbury Road, Birkenhead.

poor trade in Oxton was blamed in 1905 for failure to deal with it. By the time of the 1908 report the continuing debit had led to the closure of the Oxton branch. The Birkenhead premises were sold to another photographer.

By 1904 Arthur and his wife Ethel had already moved to 3, Silverbeech Road, Liscard, overlooking Central Park and this was my Dad, Gordon Priestley's, family home from his birth there in 1908.

Arthur Priestley, volunteer in the Great War.

War was again attributed some of the blame in the 1914 accounts but each year previously working losses had been incurred and directors had voluntarily and consistently taken reduced salaries. By the time of the report for 1919 a series of modest annual profits had reduced the debit account to £133 pounds 3 shillings and 4 pence. In the same year Fred Jefferies of Seven Kings, London joined the company, with a seat on the board.

In the 1922 report the secretary, by then James Priestley, announced a profit which wiped out the debt, but this trend was short lived and losses built up again throughout the rest of the 1920's. Regular mention is made of the contribution to this state of affairs by the depression in Merseyside's industry at the time, but this is always alongside a continued resolve to attract new business.

In 1936 Fred Jefferies agreed to undertake outdoor work at an agreed rate instead of a fixed salary. During that year, Fred had established a new business of his own [not photographic]. The last report is for 1937 and continued losses were announced. The 44th annual general meeting minutes, dated 31 March in the following year, made no mention of the company's acceptance of the voluntary liquidation, which was to follow in 1939. The last dated item is a resignation letter from Fred Jefferies [23/11/38]. The book ends abruptly here with no formal recording of the end of the company other than the auditor's final report in a separate document.

Arthur Priestley, photographer, in his studio.

The Wallasey News, dated the 19th November 1938, announced the company's forthcoming closure

This "firelight effect" picture of Arthur's son Gordon as an infant is the only example of any experimentation with colour.

with the tribute, "Locally it has for many years been regarded as an institution and genuine regret will be felt, especially amongst the older generation, at its passing".

This article also makes the point that, at the end, the business was the sole survivor of those artist photographers at work in the area, when they started off on Merseyside in 1884. Interestingly, there is mention also of the existence in company archives of 3,000 photographic views and all the portrait negatives [which were to be offered for sale to sitters] taken since 1922. Further mention of this "unique collection" was made when the Wallasey News announced Arthur Priestley's death on the 4th May 1940.

Arthur's only son Gordon with Janet Priestley [formerly Whitaker], taken around the time of their wedding in 1936.

The Falkland Road Studio

In a conversation with my Dad shortly before his death, which I recorded, he described clearly his recollections of the studio at 1, Falkland Road. The house had a reception area inside the entrance, where sample photographs were exhibited. Down the main corridor to the left was a dark room and on the right 2 vestibules, before the studio itself was reached. The studio was about 20 feet by 14 feet and it contained chairs, toys and other props as well as backdrops of various kinds. It was centrally heated and lit by electricity. The second floor was a work room, including dark room facilities, where proofs were prepared to send to the "sitters", as the customers were called. There were up to 9 or 10 people working at the studio, including an assistant called Harry Jones, who in turn had his own helper and also Fred Jefferies who joined the firm as "new blood" after the First World War and who stayed throughout until 1938.

The studio was used for individual appointments, family gatherings, for example following bereavements and for the meetings of various groups, including that of my Dad and his friends, who called themselves the Aspen Club.

Priestley and Sons took a regular advertisement in the top right hand corner of the front page of the Wallasey News and for some years they were the

The studio premises of Priestley and Sons, Photographers, at 1, Falkland Road, Wallasey.

official photographers to Wallasey Corporation. Amongst their assignments for the local authority, was a series of pictures of the imposing houses that overlooked Liverpool Bay at New Brighton, prior to the construction of the King's Parade promenade.

Arthur Priestley was also official photographer to the White Star Line for a time and a number of these shipping and riverside scenes still exist, amongst others taken in a range of north west locations, including Wallasey, the city of Liverpool, Cheshire and North Wales. Activity was split between these outdoor assignments and portrait photography at Falkland Road. From "Silverbeech", as Dad always called it, Arthur had a 10 minute walk to the studio, a return trip at lunch time for "dinner and 40 winks" and then back to Egremont for his afternoon appointments.

At the studio a showcase was erected on the Brighton Street side of the building to show off some of the photographs. Some of these were of ocean liners, taken from the ferry boats, often with the co-operation of the captains of the vessels, who knew Mr Priestley by name, so they would steer a course, where possible, to improve his chances of getting a good shot. From the river Arthur recorded the gradual addition of the "3 graces" to the increasingly impressive Liverpool waterfront.

Back at the studio, Fred Jefferies, who, as well as taking on many of the outside commitments, was helping the firm advance with his electrical expertise. My Dad described Fred as "a character, good at his job". Fred rigged up a series of new lamps, hung on overhead wires and accompanied by some very heavy cabling, but when the system was first tried it blew the main fuse at the junction box in Church Street and put out the lights at the Town Hall. It was set up again for the next day, but with the same unfortunate result, before more substantial fuses were installed and there were no more problems.

The Falkland Road premises were eventually sold in about 1947 to a family who wanted to set up a guest house.

Selection of the photographs and organisation of the book

With only 4 exceptions [the framed daguerreotype style image and one smaller positive on glass from the early days in Huddersfield and 2 experimental firelight effect prints of Gordon Priestley as an infant], all the surviving photographs in the collection are single copy monochrome prints. They vary in size from those that formed the basis of miniature cartes de visite, through various measurements from 6 inches by 4 up to large Priestley family portraits printed on thick card, which are 14 ½ by 9 ½. They mostly have a glossy finish on thin photographic paper but there are some matt surfaces and the thickness and finished quality of the prints does vary.

All the photos have been stored out of the light, some in albums, but most loosely in a series of envelope card files. They remained unsorted until the preparation of this book. Catalogues recording their existence survive and they include mention of the vast number of pictures of which there is no trace.

My Dad always believed that on the business's demise in 1939 a collection of original glass plates was installed into archives at Liverpool Museum, where, he thought, it was destroyed by bombing during the Second World War. Enquiries made recently did not yield any further evidence of the company's work being housed there.

Gordon never had any inclination to make use of the prints in any way, other than to readily lend batches of photos out on request, with his customary good nature and generosity, to anyone interested in borrowing them, including some specifically for research purposes.

As a result of his kindness a number of valuable prints were lost from the collection, though this never seemed to worry him. I even managed to persuade him to claim back one or two groups of prints, where they had been borrowed for some time, but in other cases, he admitted, they were never likely to be returned.

It is likely that most of these images have never been published before. These pictures are mostly scanned from the single copies in the collection, which have been lying in files for the last 70 years. They offer a fascinating insight into life on Merseyside and other parts of the North West, from the Victorian period up to the approach to the Second World War.

A fraction of the original pictures, about 500 prints, survive in the Priestley collection plus those in the Wirral Museum, which received a substantial donation of more than 80 prints in 2006 from another source. Most of these particular images can be accounted for by cross referencing with documented lists, as having been sold by the company at an early, but undisclosed, date.

There are also a number of broadside views of ships in the Mersey, which belong to various museum archives in Liverpool and are likely to have been commissioned by, or simply sold to, the shipping companies.

Clearly photographs from the Wirral Museum collection may have already been published elsewhere. About half of the total number of images available is present in this book. Choices have been made on the basis of avoiding duplication or similarity, though there are relatively few in this category. Others have been discounted because of faintness or fading, again relatively few. Largely though, a personal choice has been made from the range of subject matter. An attempt has also been made to include most of the really early pictures, from before 1895.

Initially, it seemed a good idea to order the photographs chronologically, so that the development of the company and its work could be traced, but the incomplete nature of the available accompanying documents meant it is not strictly possible. Not all of the photographs have an index number and even fewer have a date. In the handwritten books that record the photographs, the first, presented alphabetically by topic, is not dated at all and the second, sorted according to index number, is mostly dated, but the entries are not all made chronologically. The book was begun after the setting up of the limited company with a body of work already in place, so that many earlier photos are listed, as simply "prior to 1895" and for many there is no indication of when they were taken, though all will be 1884 onwards. The documents list literally thousands of missing photos.

In some cases there are gaps in the indexing sequences, where numbers are lacking, yet the photos exist. There are occasional instances of the same number being used twice in the documentation. Additionally, there are pencil marks on the back of some of the photos, where other people have tried to identify them later using the available records. In doing so, confusion has been further compounded by the introduction of obscure and unexplained numbering systems.

The remaining collection does not include any photographs of individuals or family groups, other than those of the Priestleys themselves. The commissions, which presumably made up the bulk of the "bread and butter" side of the business, namely portraits, weddings and other special occasions have obviously been thought of throughout as a separate entity. There is no reference to them in the surviving documentation. The record books show lists of prints made in each year from 1895, when the system started, to accompany the setting up of the limited company, with a gap of 6 years from 1914 to 1920 and only spasmodic entries in the 1920s and 30s. The impression given is that the special assignments or personal interest photos dropped off somewhat after the First World War, as the company concentrated on more basic fare to try to ensure its survival.

The photographs do, however, fall fairly naturally into a number of easily recognisable spatial categories. There are photographs taken in Liverpool, on the River Mersey, many in Wallasey and a few elsewhere on the Wirral. The opening of the Manchester Ship Canal is well documented in a dedicated album of prints. A well defined collection about the embarkation of troops for the Boer War provides another section. There is a handful of pictures from elsewhere, considered to be outside the scope of this book. These include prints of Cheshire, North Wales, Stratford-Upon-Avon and Malvern and some images from North Africa which were acquired at some stage, but were unlikely to have been taken by the company. In this last album it is not clear which are Priestley photographs and which are images Arthur collected from elsewhere.

Post script

It was clearly a struggle from year to year for the family and its employees, giving up proportions of expected salaries, hoping and planning for improvements and repeatedly being disappointed by annual financial results. For decades they worked at it, a closely related, tight knit group. They must have been so proud to have been the big name photographers of their time in the town, but, behind the scenes, no doubt content to keep the wavering fortunes of the company close to their chests. They were then and still are, rightly praised for their achievements and they have left us with some fascinating and irreplaceable images.

Many Wirral residents of today still remember Priestley and Sons, Photographers, with affection and I am very grateful to have received personal stories of trips to the studio to record a big day in a number of young lives. Priestley photos of the area I've not seen before have been brought to my attention, by kind residents with fond family memories and a shared appreciation of their local history. I am particularly grateful to correspondents who have gone to the trouble of ensuring copies of these valued, personal possessions and accompanying anecdotes have reached me.

Captions for the photographs

I have taken the captions as directly as possible from the photos themselves and the original information that accompanies the collection, adding only minimal extra comment in brackets, where I think it might be useful.

Chapter One

WALLASEY AND DISTRICT

Old Seacombe Ferry, prior to 1886
[making it one of the earliest photos in the collection]

Seacombe Ferry, before 1887

October gales, Egremont, 1889

*Mona Cottage, Liscard,
in the snow, 8/1/1892*

*Seaview Road,
28/2/1893*

*Seaview Road,
Wallasey, 28/2/1893*

Seaview Road, 28/12/1893

*Seacombe Ferry,
prior to 1895*

Wallasey Grammar School, prior to 1895

*Claremount Road, Wallasey,
looking towards the church, prior to 1895*

*Mariners' Home,
prior to 1895*

*Water Tower and St
Alban's Church, Liscard,
from the Model Farm,
Rullerton Road,
prior to 1895*

*Water Tower, Liscard,
prior to 1895*

The Noses, New Brighton, [showing] Bow of Ark, prior to 1895

Palace, Winter Gardens, New Brighton, from the Fort, prior to 1895

New Brighton, from the Fort, prior to 1895

Egremont Pier and cottages, water rough, prior to 1895

Egremont Promenade from the pier balcony, prior to 1895

Sandon Promenade, Egremont, looking towards Seacombe, prior to 1895

*Egremont Promenade
and pier,
prior to 1895*

*Ships on the Mersey,
from Guinea Gap,
prior to 1895*

*The Palace,
New Brighton,
prior to 1895*

*Pavilion,
New Brighton,
from the fort,
prior to 1895*

*Bon Marche,
New Brighton,
Bank holiday,
prior to 1895*

Egremont Pier, low tide, prior to 1895

New Brighton Pier, high tide, prior to 1895

*Guinea Gap,
from top,
prior to 1895*

*Guinea Gap,
from bottom,
prior to 1895.*

Icicles at Rock Point, New Brighton, 14/1/1895

Pond, Model Farm, Rullerton Road, 13/2/1895

ICE ON THE MERSEY AT EGREMONT. FEB. 14TH 1895.

Ice on the Mersey at Egremont, 14/2/1895

ICE ON THE MERSEY AT EGREMONT. FEB. 14 1895.

New Brighton from the pier, showing the Parade, Bank Holiday, 1895

Mariners' Home, from the river, 5/7/1895

Seacombe Hotel, Seacombe Ferry, October 1895

*Rugby Match next to
Victoria Steam Flour Mills,
January 1896*

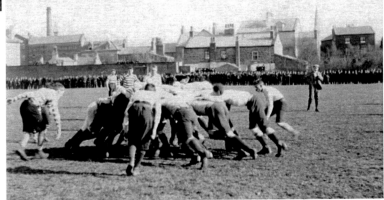

The Gala, Central Park, 25/5/1896

Rugby Match versus Manor,
1897

*The Old Bridge,
Egremont Ferry,
10/3/1897*

*Trees in Seaview Road,
Liscard,
as portion of
private road,
1897*

New Brighton Tower, Egremont Promenade, during construction, May 1898

Egremont Promenade, during construction of the tower,
New Brighton, May 1898

Seacombe Landing Stage, 1898

Seaforth and Pier from New Brighton Tower, looking NE, August, 1899

Guinea Gap, Seacombe, 26/9/1899

Vale Park,
Liscard,
1901

*Somerville House,
Poulton Road,
17/7/1902*

*Junction of
Seaview Road
towards Liscard Road,
19/8/1902*

Seacombe Promenade, 2/9/1903

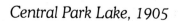

Central Park, Liscard, 6/6/1904

Central Park Lake, 1905

The Andrew Gibson Memorial Home, Egremont, Cheshire, 10/6/1907

On the Sands, Summer, 1907

Seaview Road, Liscard, 17/6/1909, towards Mount Pleasant Road

*Seaview Road,
Liscard,
1909*

Grove Road, Wallasey, 1911

*The Palace,
New Brighton,
5/6/1912*

Victoria Road and Pier, New Brighton, 5/6/1912

Egremont Ferry,
11/3/1913

43

Promenade and Victoria Gardens, New Brighton, 17/4/1913

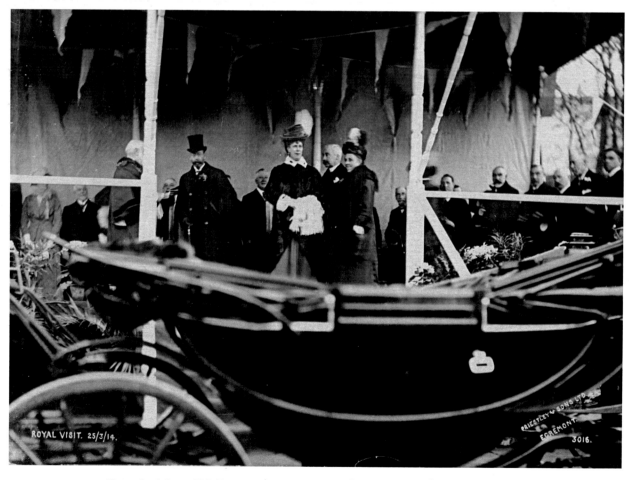

Royal visit to Wallasey, reception, Central Park, 25/3/1914

Old Boot Inn, Wallasey Road, 1925

Golf House, The Grange, August 1927

*Red Noses,
New Brighton,
August 1927*

*Vale Park,
August 1927*

*Lighthouse,
New Brighton,
August 1927*

Harrison Drive, Storm, 1927

*Harrison Drive,
Storm Havoc,
29/10/1927*

*Storm,
Harrison Drive,
29/10/1927*

Vale Park
[possibly September 1927 and no later than the mid 1930s]

Arthur Priestley was commissioned by Wallasey Corporation to take a series of pictures of the large houses in New Brighton that overlooked Liverpool Bay, prior to the construction of the King's Parade embankment and promenade in the 1930s. He took his photographs on a series of snowy days in February 1931 [the 3rd, the 24th and the 27th of that month]. This group of pictures was rescued from a skip, following refurbishment of council premises in the 1960s. For their inclusion, I am indebted to local resident and historian, Dave Jones.

New Brighton Pier, by night, 1931

Wallasey Church, Old Tower and Rectory, 21/11/1932

New Brighton Promenade, 7/8/1933

Marine Park,
New Brighton

Railwaymen's Convalescent Home, Leasowe

New Brighton

*Mother Redcap's,
Mr Kitchinman's House,
Egremont Promenade*

*Cottage at the top of
Church Lane,
Late Back Church Street*

*The front at the Magazines,
from the Foreshore,
looking south,
undated*

The last 3 photos in this section are from Birkenhead. There are surprisingly few images from elsewhere on the Wirral, perhaps reflecting the practical difficulties and the expense of transporting photographic equipment around on the roads at that time.

Birkenhead from "The Arno", Oxton, June 1905

The Irving Theatre, Argyle Street, Birkenhead

See-saw on Arno,
Oxton, 1905

Chapter Two

THE RIVER MERSEY AND SHIPPING

These first 4 fascinating early pictures in this section are at the beginning of a separate album, with a distinct and different numbering sequence and style. They are accompanied by some comments in pen to identify the main characters, but it is not clear whether they are strictly Priestley photographs or not.

Teutonic, 1887, at Spithead, Lady Claud Hamilton [second from the left], Lord Leighton [third from the left], Lord Claud Hamilton [centre], Lord Charles Beresford [right]

*King Edward 7th [when Prince of Wales]
preceded by German Emperor, 1887*

*Duke of Clarence, Prince Henry of Prussia, Prince of Wales,
German Emperor, Thos Ismay [White Star]*

Band of "Indefatigable",
Band Master, Chaplain,
School Master

*Great Eastern, beached, prior to 1895.
[Brunel's famous steamship was beached off New Ferry
in September 1888,
having been towed from the Clyde by tug]*

Yacht Mimosa, 1889

City of New York, October 1890

Yacht Iverna, RMYC Regatta, 1894

Yachts Britannia and Satanita at the Bar Lightship R.M.Y.C. Regatta, 1894

*Yachts Britannia
and Satanita,
R.M.Y.C. Regatta,
1894*

*H.M.S. Gorgon,
prior to 1895*

*City of Rome,
prior to 1895*

*Ferry boat Violet,
prior to 1895*

*Seafarers,
prior to 1895*

*Ferry boat Primrose,
prior to 1895*

*Ferry boat Snowdrop,
prior to 1895*

*Ferry boat Primrose,
prior to 1895*

The Music Room, S.S. City of Rome, at anchor, prior to 1895

Saloon, S.S. City of Rome at anchor, prior to 1895

*S.S. Teutonic,
underway,
prior to 1895*

*Flat in a breeze,
prior to 1895*

S.S. Alaska Guion, prior to 1895

Liverpool Landing Stage, prior to 1895

*A Mersey Barrow,
prior to 1895*

Ferry boat Violet, prior to 1895

Ferry boat Heatherbell,
prior to 1895

Mersey Ferry "Snowdrop",
prior to 1895

S.S. City of Rome, at anchor, prior to 1895

Ice on the Mersey,
14/2/1895

*R.M.S. Teutonic [White Star]
at Landing Stage,
Liverpool,
26/6/1895*

*Fishing boat,
1/6/1896*

S.S. Umbria, Cunard, The Queen's birthday, 1899

R.M.S. Oceanic,[Sold Cunard White Star], August 1899

*Egremont Pier in the foreground, New Brighton Pier in the background,
Evening on the river, September 1899*

*Yachts Clarissa, Velvie and Chiquita,
[presumably also from an R.M.Y.C. regatta of the 1890s]*

S.S.Oceanic, berthed at South Side, Huskisson Branch Dock no' 1, 12/8/1902

R.M.S. Teutonic, King's Visit, 19/7/1904

H.M.Y. Victoria and Albert, leaving Liverpool, 19/7/1904

R.M.S. Lusitania, at the Landing Stage, Liverpool,
[not dated, but there is a reference to a picture taken of the Lusitania
on August 27th 1907]

*Dredger Tulip at work,
New Brighton,
Wallasey Ferries,
1911*

*The Great Frost,
the Mersey at Garston,
February, 1895*

THE GREAT FROST FEB. 1895.   THE MERSEY GARSTON.   1009

In dry dock

S.S. City of Rome, at anchor

Luciana

Teutonic

Early submarine, Alfred Dock, Birkenhead

Chapter Three

LIVERPOOL

Liverpool Landing Stage,
prior to 1895

Liverpool Exchange Flags, prior to 1895

Lord Street, Liverpool, prior to 1895

St Peter's Church Pro Cathedral, Liverpool,
prior to 1895

Duke of Northumberland, George's Dock, Liverpool, prior to 1895

*Wellington Monument,
Liverpool,
prior to 1895*

Liverpool Landing Stage and Floating Bridge, April 1895

Liverpool Exchange Flags, July 1895

Church Street, Liverpool from Parker Street,
April 1897

Liverpool Pier Head, 1897

Floating Bridge, Liverpool Landing Stage, 1902

Chapter Three

TROOP SHIPS

Embarkation for the Boer War from Birkenhead and Liverpool

The Gordons off to the Cape, November 1899

Imperial Yeomanry, S.S. Winifredian, 28/1/1900

Imperial Yeomanry, S.S. Winifredian, 28/1/1900

Embarking Horses on S.S. Afric, Liverpool, 11/2/1900

*8th Batallion, Imperial Yeomanry, on S.S. Afric, W.S.[White Star]
Liverpool, 11/2/1900*

*8th Batallion, Imperial Yeomanry, on S.S. Afric, W.S.[White Star]
Liverpool, 11/2/1900*

*S.S. Montrose,
Elder Dempster and Co',
23/2/1900*

R.A.M. Corps Embarking at Birkenhead, 23/2/1900

Transport, S.S. Montrose, Elder Dempster and Co', 23/2/1900

Cymric, Transport, 23/2/1900

GROUP OF VIII BATH IMPERIAL YEOMANRY ON S.S. AFRIC (WHITE STAR) LIVERPOOL FEB. 11TH 1900. Nº 2036.

*Group of 8th Batallion,
Imperial Yeomanry,
on S.S. Afric, [White Star],
Liverpool,
11/2/1900*

"A Quiet Game",
Transport, S.S. Montrose,
23/2/1900

Cymric, Transport,
23/2/1900

Embarking Horses on S.S. Cymric,
28/2/1900

Troops for the Boer War, Mongolian, 1901

*Troops for the Boer War,
S.S. Montrose, 1901*

Troops for the Boer War, Mongolian, 1901

Troops for the Boer War

Troopship R.M.S. Majestic [at Liverpool Landing Stage]

Troops embarking from Liverpool for South Africa

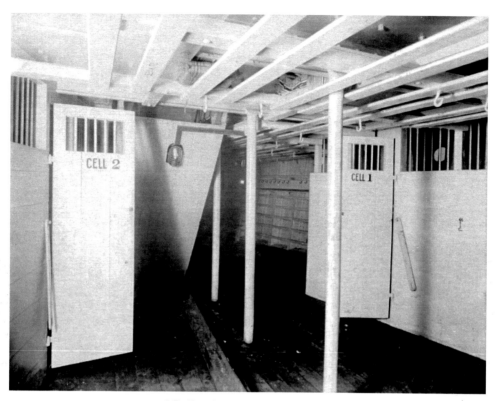

[Cells aboard troop ship]

Troop ship R.M.S. Majestic

*[Gun carriages
lifted aboard ship]*

Off to the War

*Troop Ship
Majestic Armoury*

Troop Ship Rapidan, Transport, In Dock

Chapter Four

THE MANCHESTER SHIP CANAL

Arthur Priestley recorded the opening of the Manchester Ship Canal in January and May 1894. This section of photographs is taken directly from the album he put together for that purpose. The order is that in which the prints have been affixed. The captions are those at the foot of each photo, or added in pencil below the pictures in the album.

Manchester Ship Canal Opening, May 21st 1894,
Y.M. Yacht Entrantress leaving Trafford Wharf for Mode Wheel

Manchester Ship Canal, Pomona Docks

Manchester Ship Canal, Trafford Swing Bridge from Trafford Wharf

Manchester Ship Canal, Trafford Swing Bridge from Salford

*Manchester Ship Canal,
Salford Dock No. 7*

Manchester Ship Canal

Manchester Ship Canal, Salford Dock

Manchester Ship Canal,
Shed in Salford Dock

Manchester Ship Canal, [Custom House]

Trafford Wharf, Manchester Ship Canal

Manchester Ship Canal, Opening January 1st 1894, S.S. Helvetia, Looking towards Salford Docks

Manchester Ship Canal, Mode Wheel Locks

Manchester Ship Canal, Opening May 21st, 1894,
H.M. Yacht Entrantress at Mode Wheel Lock

Manchester Ship Canal,
Mode Wheel Lock,
S.S. Standing

Manchester Ship Canal, Fairy Queen

Manchester Ship Canal, Barton

*Manchester Ship Canal,
Barton Aqueduct*

*Manchester Ship Canal,
Barton Aqueduct [interior]*

*Manchester Ship Canal,
Barton Aqueduct from
Upper Canal*

Manchester Ship Canal, Barton Bridge and Aqueduct

Manchester Ship Canal, Mode Wheel Locks, Fairy Queen

*Manchester Ship Canal,
Irlam,
High Level Bridge*

*Manchester Ship Canal,
Coal Tip at Partington*

Manchester Ship Canal, Opening, January 1st 1894, Lady Bessie leaving Latchford

*Manchester Ship Canal,
Opening,
January 1st 1894,
The Norseman
leading from Latchford*

*Manchester Ship Canal,
Opening,
January 1st 1894,
Ferry boat Snowdrop
leaving Latchford*

Manchester Ship Canal, Latchford

Manchester Ship Canal,
Latchford High Level Bridge

Manchester Ship Canal, Panoramic, [Widnes-] Runcorn Bridge

Manchester Ship Canal, [Widnes-] Runcorn Bridge

121

Manchester Ship Canal, Weston Point from locks

*Right: Manchester Ship Canal,
Weston Point and Weaver Canal*

M.S.C.   WESTON POINT AND WEAVER CANAL.   P.W.S 905.

Manchester Ship Canal, Weaver Sluices

Weaver Canal, Ellesmere

Manchester Ship Canal, Mount Manisty

125

Manchester Ship Canal, The Chairman's yacht, first trip up the canal

Manchester Ship Canal,
S.S. Fairy Queen,
leaving Eastham

Manchester Ship Canal, General view of Eastham Locks

Manchester Ship Canal, Eastham Locks

Manchester Ship Canal,
H.M. Yacht Enchantress,
at Eastham

Manchester Ship Canal,
Eastham Entrance

Manchester Ship Canal, Gunboat Speedy at Eastham

Manchester Ship Canal, Gunboat Seagull at Eastham

Liverpool Landing Stage

Acknowledgements

Andrew Flynn, Features Editor, and Tony Pogson, Huddersfield Daily Examiner.

The archivists, Huddersfield Public Library.

John H Rumsby, Museums Collections Manager, Tolson Memorial Museum, Huddersfield.

Constantia Nicolaides, National Portrait Gallery London.

Emma Challinor, Archivist, William Meredith, Archivist and Ava Wieclawska, Records Manager, Wirral Museum, Hamilton Square, Birkenhead.

Paul Keogh, Senior Library and Information Assistant, Libraries and Information Services, City of Liverpool.

Anne Gleave, Curator of Photographic Archives, National Museums, Liverpool.

Harmony Lamb, Library Assistant, Special Collections and Archives, Sydney Jones Library, University of Liverpool.

Jennifer Done, Information Officer North, Wallasey Central Library.

Dave Jones, New Brighton resident and local historian, for rescuing prints that would otherwise have been destroyed and for allowing me to use them in this book.

Ben Pedlar, The Masque Theatre, Birkenhead.

Huddersfield and Wirral residents - Mrs Patricia Kew, Miss W. Rooksby, Eric York, Lynn W. Free, Hazel Askham, Gill Lewis, Mrs Eliza Ivison, Mrs Freda Burke, Mrs Eileen Dorrity, Rebecca Robinson, Jackie Smith.

Kenneth Burnley for his advice, encouragement and practical assistance.

Christine Priestley, for her patience and support throughout.